On Our Way To HeLL

Polite Disclaimer:

This book is intended for those who have an interest in eternal matters. It is written with love for mankind and as way to shed light on our reckless behaviour that will ultimately leads to eternal hell. I know that there are many in our world that claims not to believe in either hell or heaven. Everyone has a right to believe whatever pleases him or her, but just remember that a day or reckoning is approaching sooner rather than later. Anyone who reads this book and finds it offensive has a right to stop if they so wish.

On Our Way to HeLL

Table of content

1.Intro:

Let's face it, just about everyone wants to go to heaven and definitely none wants to end up in hell. Incredibly but unsurprising this also includes even those who have loudly declared and continue to do so both privately and publicly that they don't care at all either about heaven or hell, "we don't believe in heaven or hell" they proclaim. Somehow deep down inside everyone's heart, there is this strong desire to go to heaven after we die. And as such many have ignorantly assumed that they will end up in heaven when death finally comes knocking at the door. Death is of course unavoidable and will in time catches up with all of us. We are at the mercy of death, surrounded by its morbid cloud from every side. Death occurs every minute of every day somewhere around the world though most of us pays very little or no attention to it. Death and its horror will one day visit you and me. One day I will take my last breath, and one day you will take your last breath. It is however not a bad thing not to be thinking continuously about or being consciously aware of death all the time, if that be the case then life itself would be unbearable. But we need from time to time to remember that death is only around the corner. We see thousands of people die each day around the world. Every moment that passes by is the moment closer to our own death. Someone once said that whatever is born is as good as dead, simply put; death is the sure way for all men. We are made of flesh and therefore will in time decay, there is no escaping from that fact. But unfortunately for many when death does finally come calling, our end abode will be very different from what we expect or hoped for. Hell is where most of us will end up when this life is over whether we realised it or not.

Majority of people who have passed the age of accountability are sadly on their unstoppable way to hell apparently without any hope in the world of avoiding it. Yes, most of us are sadly hell-bound. Hell will be our final, final destination, our eternal home for all eternity. And it does appear as if we are made to end up there, powerless to avoid it and are by nature children of hell, predestined for that end but why?

2.Let us look at hell

Hell is a place that most of us associate with extreme eternal pain and suffering, and we are right to have made that association. In fact, our view of hell is quite modest compared to the real reality of it. I cannot explain to you just how bad or terrible hell really is using my finite human mind and understanding, it is impossible for us human beings to even begin to fathom hell or comprehend its awfulness, let alone fully articulate or appreciates just how bad it is. Nothing on our side of life compares to it or comes close to it. We have nothing in our present physical realm of reality to draw from to help us understand just how dreadful hell really is. All we can say for certain is that hell is worse than our entire worst imaginations put together and we would all do well to avoid it. Hell is truly a terrible place, and this cannot be over emphasized, and it should really be our aim in this life to avoid it. In fact, all our efforts and power should be directed towards avoiding it at all costs but when one looks at the world today it is impossible to see anyone even paying attention to this most pressing concern.

We all seems indifferent to the reality of hell and are just happy to carry on with life as normal just the way we desire, hoping that somehow when this life is over we would end up in heaven. It is a beautiful thought that most of us have that we would somehow or magically end up in heaven when this life is over. When someone dies, people almost always assume that they have gone to heaven even if they hadn't pay any attention to this while alive. People conjures up all kinds of images of their loved ones who have departed long ago from this life, somehow in heaven and always looking favourable down upon them. But this is a wish that most of us have in our inner selves, it is the desire that we all seek after, and this drives our hope that one day somehow miraculously, we also would end up there as well. This of course is an illusion or at best wishful thinking because the reality for many will be very different indeed. You would be hard pressed to find anyone who would openly admit that when they die, hell would be their final home and are looking forward to it. Even the most corrupt person among us somehow thinks they are good enough for heaven. Well, I got some news for you; no one is good enough for heaven. There is not a person alive or dead who is good enough to deserve heaven, anyone who would end up there would do so by Grace. Everyone who is going to heaven already knows about this because people do not end up in heaven by accident or default, they do whatever is required of them to reach this most wonderful and beautiful destination.

3.Why are so many heading there?

So why would anyone end up in hell for that matter, considering how terrible a place is? Well for many, the problem is not that we are fond of hell, as we have already shown; we all love to go to heaven and not hell. Most people at least those that I know, agree on one thing, we all love heaven and hate hell almost without exceptions. Now the question is if we all love heaven, why then are so many of us heading to hell though we deride the place? The problem lies not in our love for hell but in what is obligatory in order to avoid it. You see the very things that are necessary to avoid hell are unfortunately the very things that most of us are unwilling to do or to put it another way, obey. Those things we love to do or are reluctant to give up are the very reason for nudging us towards hell. It's a conundrum.

The way to hell is paved with the irresistible stuffs that we all love to indulge in and not prepared to give up!!!=

To avoid hell, a change in our ways of living, our lifestyle is needed or required if we are to have any hope of shunning hell, something that sadly is against most of our wishes and desires in this life. Avoiding hell requires a change in our way of lives, being subject to Someone, being obedient and putting that Someone above yourself, avoiding hell is about self-sacrifice, living for Someone and trying to please Him daily, something that is hard if not impossible for us to do, especially so today. For today we see a great libertarian movement, one that puts more emphases on pleasing self and self-indulgent, a sort of me-me society. This overarching libertarian movement includes all so-called progressive alliances or movements, and the left, and all those who are vehemently promoting all kinds of fleshly lifestyles and lusts. People are constantly being told that they are free and independent and so can go on and practice whatever their heart's desires. Nothing is off limits for these groups as long they want it, they'll campaign for it until they get it, but all the while claiming to be free but in reality, being enslaved by their own wishes and desires, living like animals led by instinct and instinct alone. They don't even try to exercise a little bit of self-control because in doing so will restrict or stop the very immorality they so eager to practice, for them whatever seems pleasing to the eye or flesh is right. And they want all human beings to live like bruit beasts whose end is the way of hell. We must always remember that without self-control, no one will go to heaven. Obedience always demands self-control and discipline, something that is sadly lacking in today's world.

The way to heaven is extremely unappealing to people today. Most of us just want to enjoy ourselves, have what we see as the good life, have a good time and are not willing to sacrifice this for anything or anyone for that matter. We simply do not fancy the idea of being subject to anyone, especially anyone who would be telling us to go against our wishes and desires. We prefer rather, those who subscribe to our own wants and lusts, hell bent on satisfying these without a care in the world of any future consequences of this wild living. "You have one life," we are told, and you need to "make the most of it", "live it to the full". It is true that we all have only one life but one day this will expire and then judgement. The fact that one day we will pass on from this life hardly ever gets any attention, after all who wants to be thinking about the afterlife when there is so much to enjoy in this life right now. Most people who are enjoying life do not have time to think about the afterlife or give any thought for faith matters, simply because they are busy enjoying and entertaining themselves. Spiritual matters are far from their hearts because their logic or reasoning is that they do not need anyone or anything in life ordering or commanding how they should leave their lives. They think they have everything and do not need help from anyone let alone someone who would insist they live and act in a certain way that is contrary to what they want. They feel completely self-sufficient, lacking nothing and therefore do not need help from anyone regardless who that Being is.

A few decades ago avoiding hell was not as daunting as it is today because most of the world or at least the western world was still in strict opposition to these senseless libertarians of today rather than the current status quo, which will only get worse in the future. Don't get me wrong; it still required a lot of will power, love and above all faith to accomplish. But today however, doing any of this has become virtually impossible due to nature of who we have become. We have come a long way since the days of morality, modesty, respect, faithfulness ect. We now live in a world of immorality, self-appraisal, self-worth or boast above anything, a world where we are continuously encouraged to put our interests, desires and wishes first to the level that today we have become obsessed with ourselves, our own image, and nothing else really matters anymore. Day after day we are constantly being told to do more of this by those who professed to be in the know either in the media including all social media or those close to us, meaning avoid hell is now an impossibility for many. These so-called expert, who also includes celebrities (who are almost always libertarians in nature) have the constant ear of the liberal biased media or those in authority and their power and influence can no longer easily be ignored or dismissed. And with the increasing power and influence of social media, in which anyone who is anything can broadcast their views and or thoughts to the entire world regardless of whether they know or understand the subject matter in question, things have got even worse. Their lectures about self-worship, self-approval, or image conscious of themselves without the care about anyone else have reach a tipping point where the truth about our very existence on earth is lost in the hearts of many. Social media videos, posts or tweets that are delivered by these so-called influencers can easily seduce any of us and as such receives the most recognitions, are read and seen the most, and attracts the biggest share of likes and comments or re-tweets. They don't call them influencers for no reason, their duty is solely to attract and seduce you and I along hell highway, so that we do not care about where we are going.

There is now constant preaching on social media, perpetuated by all of us. We the people are the consumers of such garbage, liking or commenting on them all the time. This has unsurprisingly attracted virtually everyone to try their luck by faking their image or how good they feel about whatever they are doing or where they are right now compounding our collective problems. "Situation right now" one of the meme often used by many on social media to let the world know what is "happening now", letting everyone knows what we are up to right now in the hope that someone would be irked enough to comment or like. These memes often change from day to day and is sometimes hard to keep up even for the most ardent social media user. Everyone is trying to post something in the hope that it will somehow go viral and be the talk for everyone. Talk of avoiding hell does not exist here. In fact, this has become almost alien to an average person just because most of us are happy to indulge ourselves in the delights of social media, enjoying reciprocal self-congratulatory messages of "likes and comments". People commenting or liking other people's posts in the hope that this would be reciprocated on their posts as well. This is now the modern drug that is enslaving and slowly but surely engulfing the world of today. Social media is so addictive that most people can't help but succumbs to its enticing lure. It seems to give us a buzz, makes us feel better and happier though any of these only offers a temporary fix, but that does not seem to bother or deter us. We keep going back again and again for more seemingly unable to satisfy our insatiable appetite for it and forgetting our real purpose in life, enshrining our place in hell for good. We are so obsessed with how we look or feel especially on the social media even though we know that is not the real truth. We go to great length to fake our current state of wellbeing just so that we can generate more likes and comments because somehow this tickles our senses. One can now live a complete online fake life hoping that no one notices. Today, we have the ability to control what aspects of our lives to reveal on social media for the world to see or know about us while at the same time concealing the rest, especially those unflattering things which has the potential of alienating friend, likes or comments online. We are careful and diligently enough to select the very best side of us to parade on social medias in a mistaken desire that our audience will believe these to be genuine or honest portions of our lives rather than heavily edited sections designed to make others envious.

Our obsession to be liked and appreciated on social medias have led many to shun making a candid comment about anything, instead we do what society, or the vocal liberals would like us to do or say. We go to great length to avoid any negative comments or dislikes that may be directed at us and so we rather not comment or like any post or picture that might be interpreted as for example discriminating or negative even if this is by one individual. We suffer from anxiety to be liked even by strangers that we would never meet in real life and seem to care more about what online people, trolls think about us more so than we do with real friends, family or neighbours ect. This is further eroding our understanding of why we are here on earth and our purpose in life.

Many people have in fact just given up trying to avoid hell without even realising it, for them what is important is getting as much out of this world as they could, to live life to the full so to speak. And still others do not see the value of trying to avoid hell at all, they just want to live and let live. It is virtually impossible today to stumble across any posts on social medias that is intended to warn us about the dangers of hell and crucially how we can avoid it. The few posts that tries to do this don't get much traction as majority of people either don't like them or comment on them, they just get ignore most of the time. Even those who profess Christianity avoid talking about hell like a plague. It is as if hell has suddenly ceased to exist. This is misleading many people to think that hell was just a mere myth and not a reality. And such they no longer see any benefit in striving to avoid hell and therefore are choosing to go to hell so to speak, whether intentionally or not it doesn't matter, what matters now is that we as society are hell bound for sure.

Our actions and thoughts are the main drivers behind our unstoppable decent into hell because we are no longer prepared to do what is compatible with heaven's call but with hell's irresistible trap-fact!

Man has chosen to go to hell=

Many in the world are here
Both the good and the great
    according to the world are here

Very few in the world are here
Only the truly faithful are here

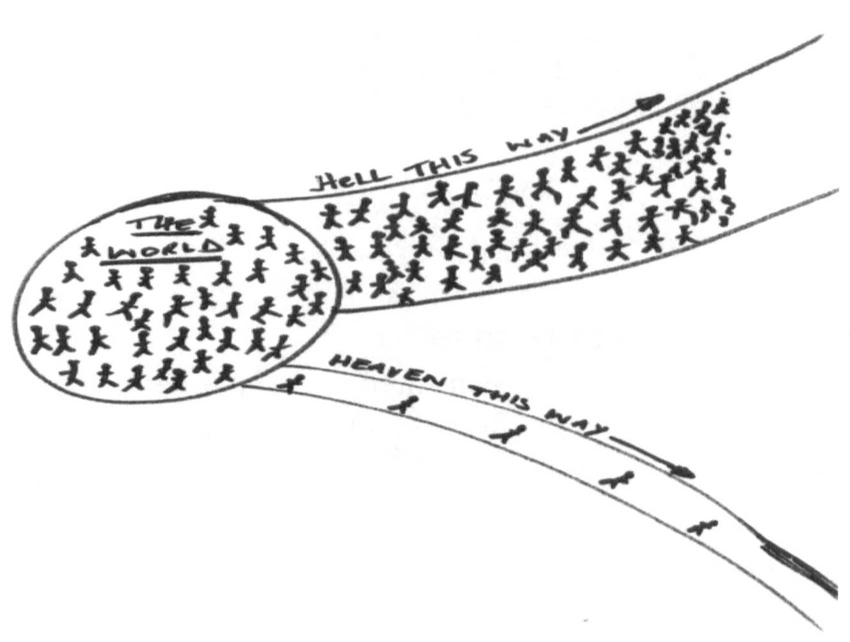

THE
WORLD
HELL THIS WAY
HEAVEN THIS WAY

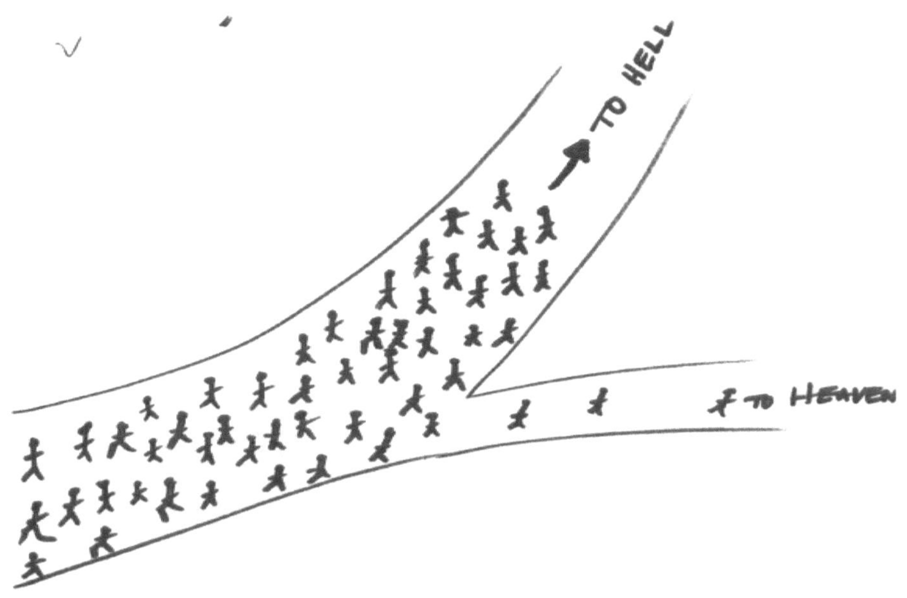

And now that we have chosen or are marching towards hell, it is necessary first and foremost that we get there. No one in their right mind would cheerfully head straight for hell with his or her eyes and ears wide open, considering how dreadful the place is. It is a said fact of life that most people who you know are on their way to hell without the knowledge of it. From the moment you are born if you are lucky enough to be born and not aborted, you are conditioned for this place by modern society. They capture you while still in the cradle and by the time most children are ten years old the game is pretty much over, already hocked on worldly entertainment, knowing all about so-called children's shows and characters. These entertainment shows are not exactly wholesome but are all over television and the Internet. There is nowhere for children to hide when growing up from worldly influences that will in time cement their place in hell when older. If only we can see what we are doing to our children eternal futures and indeed ours, it would become painfully clear that we are getting lost for ever and that we have at the very least stop or change course. So, what is it that is blinding us so complete, that we fail to perceive what is clearly ahead? What is it in this hell highway that is so powerful that we are prepared to forsake a righteous path in favour of it? What is there that is so luring or tempting that we continue to head hell-wards seemingly without any care in the world?

Hell is littered with the goodies to satisfy even the greediest among us=

Our eyes and ears are the two most critical senses that we possess. These two senses would under normal circumstances alerts us from any impending or approaching doom or danger while it is still afar off. You see danger approaching, for example a car hurtling out of control towards you; you get out of the way or take cover. You hear of any an unfamiliar sound or any sound you associated with danger from afar of you take notice and if necessary, takes evasive action. These things are hard wired into all of us so that we may live long here on planet earth, it is part of our natural survival instinct. So why are we not perceiving or rather harkening to the obvious dangers that are littered along on this hell highway? Are our eyes and ears letting us down considering that we are continuing to tread down this hell highway? Our eyes and ears seem no longer capable of helping us to avoid danger or stay clear of it. Our senses should naturally be alerting us of the approaching danger, but it appears our eyes are now so blind and ears so deaf that we are happy and quite content to continue down the same dangerous road with all the eternal consequences that lies ahead.

So, why are we so content to continue down the same hell's highway when it is obviously the wrong road to be in? The warning signs are all there, clearly visible for all to see (at least for t hose who want to see them) and loud enough for anyone to hear (for those who want to hear them). At the very least we should be shrewd enough to perceive or harkens to these obvious dangers and change course, so why don't we seem to care in the face of all these alerts and warnings. It does not seem to make sense or indeed bother us that we are getting lost. How come so many people in the world are happy and content even though we are getting lost on the road to hell?

 The answer lies somewhere inside each and every one of us, in what we really love, lust after, our wishes and desires, the very things that drives all our thoughts and actions in this life. For when it comes to going to hell, we the people are our own worst enemy. We are openly in love with the very things that are responsible for the condemnation to eternal hell. You see the very things that we desire after in this life are the very things that are in so many ways responsible for luring us towards hell so that we do not see or lose sight of the fact that we are moving in the wrong direction, heading toward eternal torment. All those things that we love so much are luring us towards hell. In fact, we love them so much that as far as we are concerned any way is now deemed acceptable if it is littered with the things we want.

Unfortunately for mankind hell's highway is bursting at the seams with all manner of attractive things many of which we have become hopeless to resist. It's like the old chicken conundrum wherein a chicken is lured by the promise of free food only to end up being on the menu. This is an ingenious way of catching a chicken without breaking a sweat by pretending to offer it free food which will fool the chicken to assume that it is getting free food without realising that this is a trap that is set up solely to ensnare and once caught there is no escape. All the chicken is thinking of is the free food on offer, help with food, but the end is the way of death, and that is exactly what hell highway is doing for us. The things we crave after that cover hell's highway are simply there as a bait and like any bait cannot be enjoyed for long. We would do well to realised that no matter how sweet or pleasant hell's high may be for now the end will be very bitter, something that we cannot endure.

Various types of lust that are aroused within us are helping to charm us hell wards and because we are so eager to satisfy them we fail to notice that the end of it all is a way of hell. Today our world is simply awash with all kinds of tempting materials; situations, people and so on, and all these are extremely seductive to all of us. These promises to offers us happiness, riches, fame and comforts, entertainment, fun and everything we could ever desire but what we fail to see is that these are like fleeting inducements designed solely to help nudge us gently towards hell without us being concerned about anything at all, going to hell deaf and blind but pampered. Today, our lives are saturated by all manner of temptations that desire all our undivided attention to fulfil. Life has always had temptations in abundance but today this has truly gone off the scale and is in danger of consuming us all. This will only get worse as more and more of us falls into this hell highway trap leaving fewer and fewer people on the outside who can alert us or warn us to change course. There are already very few people in our world that dare speak up or are ready to warn anyone that is on this wrong road, the road to hell. Most folks around us today are not interested or concerned about the direction of travel, which we have taken; they are just content to see the status quo and would never warn let alone stop anyone though they are getting lost.

If you see a blind person walking straight onto oncoming traffic or walking towards a cliff edge what would you do? Most people will try their very best to stop that person because the dangers ahead are all too obvious to all. So why aren't we eager or rather go out of our way to stop humanity from getting lost for all eternity. Instead we are busy helping each other, encouraging one another down this hell road without any concerns. When was the last time you heard someone suggest to you to stop and think carefully of where you are going when this life is over? People don't talk about such things anymore, it has become like a taboo, as if hell no longer exists. Hell, still exists and if we are not careful on how we conduct ourselves in this life, we will all end up there. It does not matter whether we acknowledge the realities of hell or not, desensitised to its awfulness or not, hell's existence will never depend on our acknowledgement or lack of it. There are those in our world who profess to be in the know proclaiming to all that once this life is over it is really the end. These get all the coverage in our liberal bias media, making their pronouncements to resonate with most people around the world. If you are in the business of warning people of the eternal dangers of hell, your voice will not be heard however loud you shout because the powers that are will do all they can to suppress it, never allowed it in the media, and will deem it too offensive and or judgemental. The left in particular are the masters of this kind of suppression because, in reality they do not want anyone to think about eternal matters at all, all they want to see is everyone focused only on the here and now, to live as if life would never end and never to give even a cursory glance about life beyond this one.

Our lives are now a far cry from just a generation ago. We now live in a world that is saturated with all kinds of creature comforts many of which we have created to help us manage our increasingly complex world. At the start of this revolution, that is the industrial revolution, it was all about making life a little easier by making machines and or equipment to help us in our daily lives. But over the years this has morphed and changed from just making necessary machines to making machines that do everything for us while we indulge in some leisure time and so forth. This need for leisure and entertainment now dominates our world and is the number one preoccupation that is at the top of those activities that are ensuring that our condemnation is complete.

It does not take much to see that the pace of change that is happening all around us is staggering. Everything that we know is undergoing exponential changes that are sometimes hard to keep up with. Material things are getting more advanced, more alluring, and better and ever more pleasing to us. Just look around you and you will see that everything it seems, is getting better and better, more appealing evermore to the eye and flesh. From humble houses to cars, computers/ smart phones, clothes, jewellery, just about every men's invention seems to be getting better, ever more advance or sophisticated and alluring evermore to us all the time. If you are in love with the world and worldly materials you have your work cut out trying to avoid hell because everything is becoming more and more desirable, and as technology develops and advances, it would seem like we are all doomed.

Just take a casual look at the discovery and subsequent evolution or development of the humble light bulb or shall I say lighting technology. It is now about 150 years since we discover that we can create light using simple materials and electricity. In the beginning of this revolution we were just excited to have managed to create light and for the next few decades all our efforts and energies were spent trying to make the light bulb last longer and be more efficient. This was a noble cause and should be commended. Today we have come a long way from the old days of carbon filament light bulb to the modern light-emitting diodes (or LED's) that are illuminating brightly our world. Producing light has never been so simple and easy to achieve. Today we are no longer so much preoccupied solely with making lighting better or more efficient but how we can use lighting technology in so many diverse ways including for example how we can use light and lighting technology to increase our mood or even entertain us and so forth. The uses of modern lighting technology seem limitless as far as we are concerned. Lighting technology has now become part of our design world and from architects to car manufactures and all tech gadgets in between, many designers, companies around the world are now actively incorporating lighting technology in their overall design to enhance desirability and enjoyment. And all this will undoubtedly help to blindside more and more people to forget the real reason why we are here in the first place. Ironic isn't it that the light that is supposed to enlighten our path is now helping to blind side us on this hell highway. In the beginning it was all about the thrill of creating light and all that it entails, but today things are going far beyond that original noble idea, to how we can engineer light and light technology to make us happy, to fulfil our lives. "The road to hell is literally paved with good intentions". And this is just looking at one aspect of technology that is rapidly changing our lives.

We are all consumed by our smart devises, to the extent that we can no longer see where we are heading...

Fewer people today are concern about the after life than say fifty years ago and this trend is only going to continue to grow. You can easily envisage a time in not so distant future where most of mankind will have their hearts and soul solely on this fleeting passing life without ever giving a thought or preparing for the hereafter. We all know that one day all of us would die and pass on from this life, but the shocking truth is that we are still completely focused on the here and now as though death will never come visit us. Have you been to the funeral lately? If you had you will be familiar with the words," he or she who had passed away is looking down on us or is now our guardian angel". This shows that even those that care not about the afterlife are also fully aware that death is not necessary the end of our existence and yet not many are preparing for this. We must remember that we do not cease to exist at death but rather enter eternity.

4.The comforts of life

There is no doubt that our lives are increasingly becoming more and more comfortable and this trend is more likely to grow for many around the world as the earth riches spread throughout the world especially in the developing world. We will soon go beyond a point of no return as humanity where all our focus and efforts will solely be on earthly matters alone, perhaps we have already gone pass this Rubicon. Over the last few decades we have witnessed an incredible rise of the middle class around the world. With this comes rising wealth for many giving many the ability to afford life little luxuries and leisure time. These few luxuries are hard to resist for modern man. Although there is still a lot of poverty, hardships and suffering around the world, we have witnessed an incredible rise of wealth around the world especially in the developing world. In my own home village in Africa for example, people are now able to afford many of the luxuries that only a few decades ago would have been a dream but today it is a reality that many are now enjoying. Some of them are now living in such comfort that they give many in the West a run for their money, quite literally. Some people from my home village are now enjoying such pleasures as playing golf, frequent holidays, eating out on a regular basis, parties, owning and driving multiple luxury cars that many in the West would not expect to see in an African village. When I was a young boy a few decades ago, seeing a car was something to behold, there were hardly any cars around on the road in our village. We used to play on the road all day long without worrying about being hit by any cars. Finding yourself in a car was like an out of the body experience and something to be forever cherished. We would spend days perhaps weeks or months talking about it. But today even if one has a luxury SUV or an expensive supercar, people no longer dwell on those for much longer, because it is no longer seen anymore as something extraordinary. How times have changed indeed. I myself have been a witness to some extraordinary social change in my life, something that could I not be foreseen when I was a child. My life has changed beyond even my wildest imagination when I was a child. As a child I would walk barefoot to school for lack of shoes but today I even I from an unknown African village can afford to fly, now that's truly remarkable isn't. But it is not just I alone; this is fast becoming true for many people from around the world. Wealth is now spreading rapidly around the world, lifting many forgotten people out of abject poverty. Many people around the world are now enjoying such luxuries that would have been unthinkable only a few years ago.

And with all this wealth, many people no longer worry about what some would call the mundane or necessities of life, food, shelter and clothing but rather can now focus most of their attention and effort on extra curricula social activities. And there is no shortage of such activities for us to indulge in once the basics of life have been taken care of. Human beings are masters of inventing activities to do with our time outside of the daily grinding for life's necessities. Entertaining ourselves is something that we are very good at. These things that we do outside of the real life's necessities are the very things that are helping us head for hell without much resistance. All the creature comforts that we have developed over the years to assist us in our daily lives are now so brilliant, so all consuming and attractive that we can no longer see where we are heading. Whether is cars, or anything that moves us from place to place, internet, television, radio, smart phones, computers or tablets, all modern conveniences and so on, there is simply no shortage of help in our modern way of life.

5.The convenience of life

Life itself is fast becoming more and more convenient, from the way we travel from one place to another, or how we shop with many things now only a click or swipe away. We now have smart television with a variety of smart function including AI, smart phones which are very handy for many functions we simply can no longer do without, smart fridges that can order our groceries, smart cars that get drive themselves, smart everything but amazingly at the same time we ourselves are becoming more and more indifferent as we continue our over reliance on technology. We have reach a point in our existence where we are letting machines to simply take over our lives for good or bad. We are allowing technology to do everything for us while we sit back and enjoy the delights and comforts of life, enjoying the ride so to speak entirely unaware of our eternal destination. Technology has now taken over our lives with our own consent for better or worse. Have you been on a public transport lately, or find yourself among a crowd, I mean everyone around is quite literally glued to their smart phones, iPads and so forth. Everyone is looking down on their smart phones or so-called tablets and some people on the buses or trains have been known to even miss their stop while busy checking their so-called smart devices.

These devises are so addictive to mankind that once hooked there is virtually no room to escape. And now with the popularity of head set, most people won't even harkens to any warning however loud, that they are heading in the wrong direction. We seem to no longer care anymore about where we are heading if the ride is comfortable, and if we have everything we think we need, if we are being entertained, if life is good, we just ride along seemingly ignorant of everything else including the obvious dangers ahead. All the warning signs that can be placed on hell's highway will never be enough for many today because we simply cannot perceive them for our eyes are now glued to our smart devises.

We are now in the process of building a new virtual world complete with human and machine inter-phase, along this road, which would undoubtedly help to sanitise everything ahead. All the awfulness of hell will be sanitised in our virtual world to become anything we want it to be. And all you will need to access in this new world is a VR set and hell will be yours without a wink. All the danger signs along this road would be invisible to anyone who is busy being entertained by their own comfortable virtual world. You can now live your entire life in virtual reality, which is no reality at all, but a false one where enticement belongs, which would damn one's soul. Nothing else matters anymore to people so long as they are enjoying themselves. Fun, fun, fun is now the only game in town. You can now take people to the very gates of hell and they would not even notice it, how sad!

We are in love with worldly things and as such destined for heLL

6.Life will seem to continue to get better and better

And as technology continues to advance our life would seems to get even better and better the closer to hell we get. It is evident that our world is becoming more and more appealing with explosions of every kind of entertainment imaginable. But worryingly for us, at the same time our moral conduct is getting worse and worse. It is as though the closer we get to hell the higher the need for us to be as immoral as possible so that we can justify our permanent place in it. We are now advocating for such immoralities that only a few years ago would have been unthinkable, thinks like full term abortions are now being actively supported and campaigned for and will be completely acceptable sooner rather than later.

7.Technology helping to send us to hell without ant resistance..

Technological advancement is happening at incredible paste. The rise of digital technologies merging with AI is today transforming every aspect of our modern life. This new cluster of technological advances is changing how we live, work and play. Physical and virtual realities of our lives are increasingly becoming intertwined and overlapping. Machines that we have created are now the new mediators of more and more of our interactions with the world and of objects around us. We are increasingly becoming over-reliant on technology to help us with everything, sadly today this now include deciding where are eternal homes should be. From our homes to work places, play and everywhere technology is improving the way we do things all the time, improving lives of so many people around the world. From manual jobs to highly skilled ones technology is improving this all the time. Technology has change changed our world and is continuing to affect and influence mundane lives of millions of people around the world. The world around us will always change but it is how we interact with changes around us that would determine how our world would look in the future.

The way we access information for example has change completely beyond even our untold imaginations. Only a few years ago it was impossible to speak directly with someone on the other side of the world face to face and in real time but today this complex interaction is commonplace. Many of us do this without giving it a second thought especially millennials. For them things like video calling or face time as it's now commonly referred to, is just an ordinary part of their daily life. It does not seem amazing to them that we can talk to each other face to face from any part of our planet. They look at all of this as if we have always been able to do so. Only a few years ago mobile phones were but a distant dream, something that belongs to science fiction but today we simply can't live without them. They have revolutionised and transformed our whole way of life doing so much more that we can ever ask for. We have now truly entered a digital age, a world of seemingly endless possibilities and there is no more going back. And this new digital world is ensuring that every hurdle is lowered, every bump smoothed over on hell's highway and that we are well taken care of especially as we get closer to hell.

Our digital world==01010101010101010101010101010101010101010

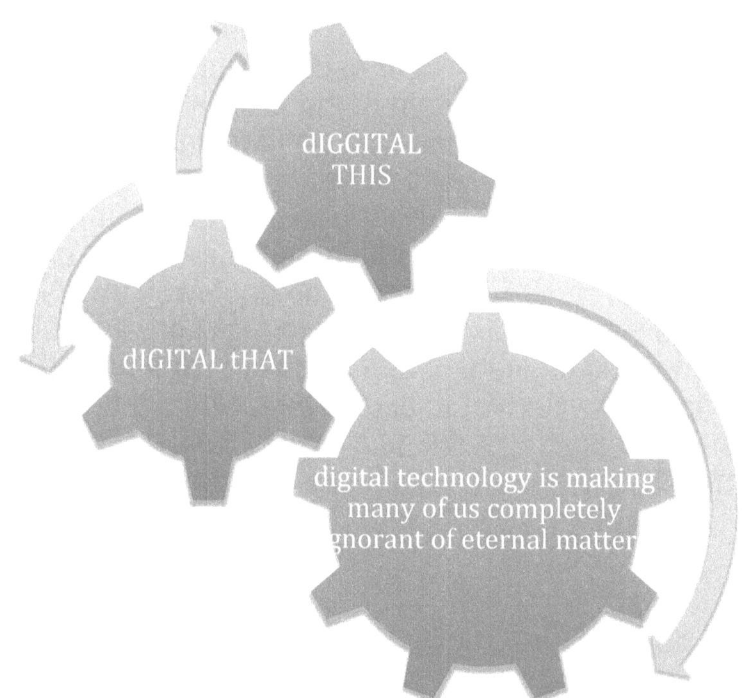

101010

Our homes are no longer just a place to lay our head or have rest from the daily grimes of life; they have now become a hub of all kinds of technologies, hotbed of all kinds of technological revolutions. Technology has revolutionising our homes beyond measure over the last hundred years. Homes are no longer the dull places so to speak but have become extremely advanced that many of the house chores can be done at a flick of a switch or a simple swipe on a smart phone. From the moment you wake up to the time you go back to back to bed there is simply no task that our modern tech world can't seem to handle in our homes. You get to be woken up gently by a nice sounding alarm on your smart phone, while the same smart phone controls and let the lights in your bedroom to comes on, open your blinds for you while the thermostat had already started heating your water and your home an hour earlier. Your bathroom can be programmed to fill your bath to the required level and temperature so that all you do is get in and start bathing right away. The bath itself is a technological marvel with the ability to soothe and massage you gently with strategically position jets of water that will take your cares and troubles away even if is for a moment. Getting out you dried yourself with an already warmed up dry towel. Brushing your teeth was once considered by many as boring chore but now can be done with advanced toothbrush that do all the work for you, all you need to do is hold it in your mouth and guide it along. It now knows how to clean your teeth to get the best results. Modern technology is simply amazing!

Once everything is finished and you are ready to go to work and face the world, you don't even have to switch of all the light in your home, or televisions etc, everything can be set so that all this are turn off at a preset time.

Homes are getting smarter all the time as technology improves. Many house chores have been made simpler and easier to perform due to improvements in technology. Mundane tasks like for example house cleaning were once considered a rather tedious and boring jobs that only the low paid should do but today machines can do this on our behalf while we chill and relax. Modern technologies has freed us from many house chores that out ancestors were unable to escape, leaving us plenty of time to enjoying and to indulge ourselves in anything we desire. We got washing machines for our laundry (they can even dry our clothes), dish washers for our utensils, Fridges that can tell us when we need to do our grocery shopping and so forth, and its not as if we need to go to the store, we can easily do our weekly grocery shopping online and it will be delivered right to the door for us. Fridges of the future will be able to alert us of what groceries are needed because they will be able to know those items of groceries that are low or have run out.

Some people are now openly talking about intelligent homes of the future which would for example be able to distinguish between family members, being able to know what kind of music you like (i.e custom music), kind of lighting required for which occasion, adjust room temperature, all this without you having to do anything. Information will simply need to be uploaded on a smart device, which one can wear, part of wearable technology, and this will contain all the information required to make this possible. This new class of technology that can be worn is already getting wide spread use by many tech fans around the world and many companies are now in a dash to develop new and exciting wearable technologies for a variety of new applications. We are entering a new uncharted phase in which our digital world seamlessly intergrades with our physical world, scary isn't it. All this by the way is necessary if we are to make it all the way to hell. We need to be distracted and blinded by as many material things/circumstances as possible on this journey to hell otherwise we might see the light and be tempted to change course.

And as everything in our modern world gets this digital treatment so is our reasoning and thinking. We now act very more like the very digital machines that we have created. Rational reasoning or thinking is now out of the way ensuring that we cannot turn back from the horrors of hell. We have taken the bait hook, line and sinker!

Our obsession to fulfil our lustful desires has as it where already cemented our place in hell. We have lost completely the understanding of why we are here in the first place because we have let our quest to satisfy our lustful desires take over us literally. We are no longer prepared to live and behave in line with anyone's ways or desires. Our very own wishes and desires now take precedent over and above anyone else's including sadly our very own Creator. We no longer care about anyone but ourselves, especially if that someone else ways of life is contrary to or in direct conflict with our own. And this has led us to become our own masters not willing to submit to anyone. To do and to act as we wish without any boundaries or barriers is to us very appealing but unfortunately this way of life has painful eternal consequences. I said this again, we have decided to go to hell, we have chosen our destiny and it seems nothing can stop us now. And we are quite happy with our choice regardless of the terrible eternal consequences that lies ahead and are not prepared to listen to anyone telling us otherwise. We are hell bound with the smile on our faces…

8. Hell what hell!!!!!

Now it seems fitting that those who have chosen hell as their final eternal destination, the worst possible place in all of human history should arrive there in style and in comfort without worrying or lacking about anything they desire or wish for. Everything we long for in this life, our needs and desires or even our lusts, you name it, it is been provided for on this rather wide hell road and we not do we have to worry about anything. The way of hell is bursting with the staff to satisfy even the greediest among us, all of our wants (notice that its not our needs or requirements), wishes and desires are taken care of. We can now sit back and pamper ourselves at will, at any time, fulfilling our every wish and desire that we could ever have, indulge ourselves without shame, practice whatever we please, believe anything we desire, no moral boundaries here to stop us from every lust. All the earthly happiness that a man could ever want seems to be catered for. We can gratify ourselves time and time again and in any way we pleases. The music that you are busy listening to is only there to serenade you down this hell highway. And this is what most of us are craving for and this goes some way in explaining why hell's highway is full to bursting by people from all walks of life. In this highway, you can be anything you want to be, be as immoral as you want, be as awful as you dare, do anything you desire, and you will still have a red carpet rolled out just for you as long as you are on this road to hell. You will be made to feel special and highly favoured, one of a kind individual. All are welcomed on this highway to hell. There is simply no discrimination; it doesn't matter what colour you are, what race you are, where you are from, male of female or whatever you call yourself, every group of people is welcomed however weird their practice or way of life is.

You can be anything you like on hell highway…all are welcomed!

murders adulteres
envious liers haters of
good

pride lies selfiesness
drunkensess

jealousies live and let live
covetous

But on heaven's way only those who surrender fully to their Creator are allowed,

The only group of people not accepted here are those who have chosen to live within moral boundaries and in accordance with their

Creator. The way to heaven no longer appeals to our lustful us and we rather end up in hell if we can satisfy all our wants now!!

It's not surprising to me nor should it be to anyone that those who are suffering the most in this life or less fortunate are more likely to go to heaven than everyone else. Don't get me wrong here, I'm not suggesting that for you to go to heaven you must suffer or be poor or destitute and if you are rich and comfortable the only way is hell. We all have equal chance to some degree of either going to heaven or hell. The choice of were we end up is completely within our hands. Everyone has a choice to decide where he or she will end up in all eternity when this life is over except for those who are either too young or mentally incapable of discerning good from evil. What I'm saying here is that those who are suffering or live in poverty in this life or seemed to have nothing or no hope are more likely to think about the afterlife and more crucially spiritual or faith matters than those whose every need is taken care of. Suffering people or those afflicted by poverty have very little if anything to look forward to in this life and are more likely to turn to faith than those who are rich and enjoying the good life. This is just the reality of who we are. Rich people or those enjoying the delights on this life simply do not have time to think about the afterlife because they have already made it, so why spend time worrying about life after death when this life right now is so good. They do not want even think for a moment to entertain matters beyond this life because they are busy enjoying themselves. For them life is full of endless opportunity to have fun, make money and enjoy. The world for them is like an oyster ready to be enjoyed at anytime of their choosing. It is only when they are faced with their own mortality that they might start to think about eternity. Most of us when faced with our own end, money or fun become unimportant or irrelevant. You can promise a terminally ill person or someone who is about to die a million dollars and still they will not be happy or satisfied with that, why? Because money however plentiful, will not give anyone life or extend it even for an hour. What that person need is life something that money can't buy. Such a person however is more likely to turn to faith matters in the hope of finding salvation. Money as we all know cannot and will not buy salvation.

The way to heaven is paved only with those things that many of us are simply not interested in or do not like for that matter. There is self-sacrifice along the way, looking to the needs of others as yourself, obedience is a must, living to please someone else and putting Him first must be your priority, your whole aim and your duty in this life must be to live for Someone else all the days of your life. Now this is hard for us to stomach, because our physical bodies are always pulling us in the opposite direction. The physical body is always wrestling against our spiritual self and for many the physical body always emerges a winner. Human beings have always find the idea of limiting our wishes and desires very difficult to do because this involves restricting ourselves from the things that our bodies wants and desires, those things that gives us pleasure or tickle us. This leaves us to act like slaves to our very own bodies; hopeless beings that are been pulled towards hell without any apparent help but why? The reason is that we don't want to take charge of our bodies because this requires self control something that has now become alien to many but rather we enjoy being carried away by various lusts our bodies so desires. We have given up trying to be the masters of our bodies, drivers of our bodies' and now have become helpless passengers. It has now become impossible for us today to bring our bodies into subjection because we prefer to "live and let live" so to speak. You have heard excuses like I was born that way; I couldn't help it and so forth. Though we know that letting our bodies takes control over us is risky at best downright deadly at worse we continue to let this continue unabated because we enjoy the lust of the flesh. We need to remember that this kind of living though gratifying has disastrous consequences both now and eternal. This way of living will damn your soul and mine for all eternity if we do not change course. Although for now it allows us to indulge every wish and desire without any limits, the end will be a sorrowful and painful one without escape. We are today so unashamedly wicked and immoral, but this sort of living is nothing new in our human history.

The way to Heaven has these in abundance

Human beings have travelled down this wicked road before. Our long history is littered with many examples of this level of immorality if not worse, from many previous generations. And this level of wickedness has appeared many times in history affecting different civilisations in different parts of the world. We should by now have already learnt from this part of our history the serious consequences of unashamedly walking down this wicked road, learning from them what happened to those who walked down this path, but we seem to have learnt nothing. It is painfully strange how history repeats itself. There is an old saying that says, "a clever person learn from their own mistakes, but a really smart person learnt from another's mistakes". But we are not prepared to learn anymore from anyone, we think those who came before us and perish along hell's highways were not smart enough and we think we are so much better or wiser than them. Today we are repeating the very errors they have made before, completely ignorant of our own fate that is surely lies ahead if we do not change course. We are not as clever as we think for who in their right mind would deliberately engaged in activity that would ultimately damn his or her soul for all eternity. We claim to be wiser today than all the generations that have existed before. We are proud and in many ways pompous, boasting what could possibly go wrong. We managed to send man on the moon; we can treat and cure many of the diseases that used to blight humanity in the past. We can travel vast distances within a very short space of time, we can see inside of the human body with amazing clarity than ever before, make computers that can handle trillions amount of data, make billions of calculations a second and all at a touch of a button.

We have made so much technologically advancement in the last hundred years that there are some among us now who believes that we are invincible. Some people have gone as far as thinking that soon we will find a way to enable us to live forever. In fact there are those who are such true believers of this madness that they are already preparing for such eventuality. We have lost all sense of eternal matters that today our entire focus in life is purely on earthly matters without even a mere glance at eternity. This is exacerbated by the fact that we have now achieved so much in every sphere of our lives than any of those who preceded us. Our achievements today dwarf any that have been achieved by any previous generations. We think we are so much better than them, for our knowledge surpasses them all. We have been able to do things that previous generation thought impossible. And yet I contend that we are no wiser than those who came before us if in the end we are still proudly walking along hell's highway they too travelled through. We simply cannot claim to be wiser than any generation before if we are still being fooled to continue down the same road they wandered in the past towards hell. I say this again, "No wise person would knowingly engage in any activity that would ultimately destroy his or her soul". One would think that we would be more smarter than any generation in the past because of our great vantage point that we can draw from, the level of wealth of recorded human history that is already behind us, we would have learnt long ago the consequences of remaining on this path but sadly no. We are carrying on down the same path that our ancestors have trodden even though they ended up being lost.

Technologies will undoubtedly continues to change our lives well into the future. Today we have online shopping that provides us with just about everything we could ever wish to buy twenty for seven meaning we are no longer restricted to shop during certain hours or days. We have now entered a truly twenty-four seven world in which day and night seamlessly flows one to another. Shopping no longer has to stop when the sun goes down. Technology is making life easier and for many more enjoyable, living life without a care in the world.

Life it seems has never been so good and comfortable. We no longer must the extreme in temperatures in our homes like our ancestors did; we can simply control temperature in our home with a simple swipe or switch. We can no longer suffer the pain of going out in any weather collecting water or firewood; our homes have all we need inside. We no longer must worry about what we will eat; food is plentiful for many especially in the West. We no longer have to worry about what we must wear, clothes are now in abundance and cheap for most. We no longer have to worry about how we would travel from A to B, we can cross the planet quite literally and in great comfort, we no longer have to worry about how to communicate with loved ones who are on the other side of the world, and many of the issues that are ancestors used to worry about have been removed leaving us plenty of time to enjoy life. Many of the diseases that blighted them are today easily treatable. So, when it comes to life, there is nothing that we seem to lack, all seems provided for. Therefore many people have mistakenly concluded that we do not need anyone to help us with anything as we are now completely self sufficient though this is false. Now free from the shackles of the past, the daily grimes of irking an existence, we can now focus all our attention on enjoying life and entertaining ourselves. In the past entertaining each other was very simple and local but today technology has changed all that.

9. Entertaining ourselves to hell

There are a lot of things in this world that would easily ensnares and captures our attentions and interests but those that purports to give us pleasure and bliss ranks amongst the most powerful and nothing does it better that entertainment. People everywhere are yearning for some form of fun and pleasure daily. Entertainment offers these in abundance.

The Entertainment has now become the most preeminent buzzword in our modern world and all society and cultures everywhere are now chasing after it. I mean who doesn't like to be entertained? It is as if we human beings have been made for that very purpose though this is not the case. Human beings takes into entertainment like ducks into water. We simply love it. We are so obsessed with it that today most of us now live for it and are prepared to go to any length to have it.

Just take a look around you today and see for yourself just how much entertainment there is. It has infiltrated every aspect of our lives and controls most of what happen in our world today. So abundant and prevalent is entertainment that very few people are managing to resist its pulling power. It is been promoted just about everywhere from television, Internet, magazines, newspapers etc. Every aspect of our lives now revolves around entertainment making it the central pillar from which every part of our lives interlinks. It truly goes into the very heart; the inner core in all of us, and this explains why entertainment is the center of everything that is helping to nudge us further towards hell. And today modern technology is enabling entertainment to go global with ease, available to billions of people twenty-four seven day and night. Any entertainer be it musician, actor/actress or sporting icon can continue to entertain the masses continuously non-stop all at the click of a button.

People throughout history have always sought after things to entertain themselves, so it's nothing new if we today are also clamoring after it. But it seems like there was always something restraining our unquenchable appetite for it. Today that restraining barrier or influence whatever it was is now well and truly out of the way leaving us to go all the way.

Over the last hundred years or so there was a steady rise in a number of different activities that we indulge in for entertainment pleasure. It wasn't until after the Second World War that this truly took off and began to permeate every aspect of life that we are now familiar with.

You see different societies and cultures have from time to time immersed themselves in entertainment but none more than the World of today. Our love affair with entertainment can be summed up by these lyrics, "Girls just wanna have fun". Indeed this expression is merely reflecting what was already happening in the World, that most of us are only interested in entertainment and pleasure of the flesh. paying no attention to eternal matters. We are not prepared to look at the eternal consequences of such irresponsible living. Consequences don't matter anymore; fun is now the ultimate universal mantra.

And now with the advent of the so-called social media, entertainment has been being taken to whole new level. People are glued twenty four seven to their smart devises enjoying limitless amounts of entertainment. New game like Pok mon go has taken over the world with millions upon millions of devoted followers chasing after the wind, following so-called virtual animated objects prepared to go even to the ends of the world, endangering their own lives and that of others, with no respect for anyone or anything, just focused on getting the Pok mon and all in the name of entertainment. No one even pause for a minute to think about what they are really doing. People are happy to blindly follow anything as long as it is entertaining, even going as far as the gates of hell as long as they are being entertained. The consequences of this blind faith is dangerous folks because it means anyone with sinister motive and easily fool people by enticing them with entertainment leading them to oblivion or even hell without them realizing it. You see entertainment has always attracted huge followers from roman theaters to new theaters of dreams.

There was a time not long ago when people had rational view of entertainment and not the current prevailing madness. Don't get me wrong here; there is nothing inherently wrong with entertainment although some entertainments are. And just because someone is being entertained or entertaining others does not necessarily means they are wrong. There are many good reasons why one would entertain others or seek entertainment. After all the word entertainment has been used in the past to indicate for example, looking after your guests. But today its meaning has well and truly changed and what we are now witnessing being done in the name of entertainment is sometimes shocking and beyond anything that could be considered normal or acceptable. Entertainment has now become like a drug that most of us are addicted to and without it we feel the urge to have it and have it now.

Today technology is helping us to indulge in our past time of entertainment that ever before. Our need for entertainment and fun has always been insatiable but today with the help of technology we can indulge in this at anytime of our choosing and anywhere n the world. Technology has changed the way we consume entertainment making it easier for us to access this even on the go. All the programmes that you love can easily be watched on demand any time of the day or night. You never have to miss anything anymore. There are box sets to watch, films/videos to watch, social medias to indulge in, music to serenade us down hell highway, sports on demand and so forth, and we are so in love with these that it is hard to imagine life without it. Human beings love entertainment, any form of entertainment. People will queue for hours sometimes days in cold and rain to get their hands on latest tickets for varying sporting and music events. We have all seen what the gadgets mad young people of today will go up to, to get hold of latest smart phones. They scramble and sometimes stampede on each other to be the first to get one. One would think that they were scrambling for something that is very important and very rare, but if they could just wait for a day or so they could simply just walk into the store without any hassle and still buy one with ease. But these people do not want to wait, even if it is for something that would look rather ancient within a year when the latest smart phone appears and the whole madness is repeated again. We are now so madly in lust with entertaining ourselves and would go to any length to achieve this.

From our very earliest beginnings, entertainment has always form part of our lives. It provided us with escapism as long as we can remember. Different societies in different parts around the world cannot help but entertain themselves. From the traditional African dances to Hollywood films, entertainment is what we do best. Today, there are a myriad of different forms of entertainments, from sports, to films to video games, the list is endless and all vying for our complete attention. To top it all there are now also many different ways of accessing entertainment, no longer must individuals have to be physically present in order to enjoy or take part but can do so in the comfort of their homes.

Accessing entertainment today is getting effortless and easier as smart phones popularities exploding around the world. Television consumption is also growing around the world. And as television become smarter, there will be more functions added that can be access to enhance the overall experience of the user. If you love entertainment you have your work cut out if you are trying to avoid hell. Social medias like Facebook and YouTube have billions of users daily. Their influencers have millions of followers and follow their every move or turn. Society is now turning to these for advice and guidance on everything including life after death. We assume that just because someone is famous on social media, somehow he or she must have special knowledge that most of us do not have. These influencers are themselves just as blind to this as the rest of us. They do not know anymore than we do even though they are famous. We need to remember that most of these influencers are famous for doing noting tangible. Most of them are famous for being famous but are there merely to entrance our need for entertainment and comfort.

Remember those heading for hell needs to be entertained, comforted and well looked after in order to distract them from the horrors that awaits on the other side of life, otherwise they might change course. They need to be blinded or seduced by as many things as possible so that they can reach hell without qualms. If the way to hell wasn't awash with the very things we crave for no one will end up there so easy. Everything you want to do or say is permissible on hell's highway, liars are there, cocks are there, back stabbers are also there, so are fornicators, murders, thieves, those who covet, proud, boasters, untrustworthy, unforgiving, unmerciful, envious, and the like, the list is almost endless. Now you can see just how wide ranging those who are destined to hell are and very few people will be able to avoid it.

I think we need to take a pause, to carefully think about entertainment and everything that goes with it. Because I'm afraid if we don't, we will all be led astray at best or worse perish without realizing it. Entertainment has such a powerful hold on us, and the only natural or smart thing to do to think carefully how best to proceed before it is too late.

10. Hell highway caters for all.

No amount of enticement, fun or inducements should be able to persuade us to join and stay on hell's highway. We should not allow things of this world to cloud our judgement about our eternal destiny after all we can only have things of this world only for a season. We need to remember that we brought nothing into this world and it's evident that we can take nothing out of it. We need to be wise enough to accept this reality and not allow the things of this world to entice us away from heaven or confuse our judgement about the meaning of our existence. We should not let the things of this world whether entertainment, power, fame or even fortune, which eventually will fade, get in the way and cause us to end up in hell away from heaven.

11. Was it worth it?

The intellect

Was it worth it oh you professor to hold on to those unproven theories or shall I say ideologies "the big bang and evolution" even though neither you nor anyone could substantiate them. You held onto this to fit your wicked narrative that there is no Creator afraid and worried that accepting His existence would require a change in your heart and therefore lifestyle. You blindly carry on this idea throughout your entire life to satisfy your own conscience and that of your peers in a desperate attempt to justifying your way of life. You rather embrace a false ideology than accept the reality of our Creator who is to be forever praised just so you can avoid conforming to His way of life. Looking back now do you think it was worth it?

The rulers

Was it worth it to you politician who in life insisted that men could do whatever they please, even going as far as changing long held and accepted moral values and norms just to be win votes and acceptance by the wicked of the world and leftist media? In life you did everything you could to win votes, accepting any and everything that those who shout the loudest wanted or desires. You never gave a straight answer to any question, rather you always gave vague so called political answer, avoiding taking a stand so that you can maintain your popularity, fearing offending the public. Was it worth it now that you are in the deepest parts of hell?

The Law changers

And to you who call yourself a judge. Why were you always on the side of evildoers, the wicked, letting them to get away with murder quite literally while at the same time condemning the innocent. You use human rights and other bogus right to justify your wicked conclusions on every judgement. When the immoral comes before your courts clearly guilty, they feared no justice because they knew the so-called justice was always on their side. All kinds of rights were always thrown at them while at the same time the real innocent receives no rights or protection at all and were condemned without defence. Was it worth it to rule always in favour of the guilty while oppressing the innocent leaving them with no one to call upon?

The liberal left

Was it worth it for you, liberal activist? You campaign for those hell-bent on evil, people with corrupt minds whose actions and thoughts are toward evil continually. You were quick to appeal to human right and others so-called rights in your quest to defend any behaviour or actions that you deemed acceptable and like to promote. Once you sets your eyes on who ever is against your way of life there was no stopping you. You stirred up culture wars with your obsession with evil, crushing anyone who stands opposed to you. And when you fail there were always the courts to run to where you knew that victory was always assured since those who sit in judgment were on your side. You thought you had the whole world under your feet, winning every judgment however wicked what you were fighting for was. Looking back now, do you think it was worth it?

Celebrities

Was it worthy it for you so-called celebrity, you who are famous, who in life practiced any and everything as long as it would make you more famous and popular? On social medias you were prepared to bare all in the pursuit of more likes and comments. You stopped at nothing endorsing any and everything that you thought the people wanted. You even changed your long held views on morally whenever challenged, in total fear of losing fans and fame. You succumb to whatever morality endorsed or practiced by those who shout the loudest fearing offending anyone. This you did, not because they were right but because you knew that going against such was career suicide, something you were not prepared to give up. Looking back now was it really worthy it to hold on to something that was passing away.

People can choose to be offended if they so desires, but the truth will always be just that regardless of who is offended. If you are offended by what is written therein that is your choice but you should not be allowed to force that on anyone.

The Rest of us

And to the rest, why did you keep silent when the liberals were running riot, when sinful acts were being elevated to goodness. All those myriads of groups whose purpose was to promote and allow wickedness on mass were given all the airtime and privileged on television and on social medias. Social media was saturated with their gospel, the gospel of the left that it seemed at times impossible to escape its influences. And anyone who appears to oppose such was treated with instant injustice while you kept your silence even though you knew what they stood for was right. Evil and wickedness became widespread and dominated the world thanks to you're your deafening silence. Was it really worth it to keep silent and look the other way?

We all should stand up to this all forms of wickedness and evil, including those we love to practice before it is too late. After all we only have one shot at life and we cannot afford to miss the mark. If we do miss the mark there awaits us all eternal regret and worse!!